TABLE OF CONTENTS

Chapter 1: Laying the Foundation

Chapter 2: Mastering the Tax Industry

Chapter 3: Essential Tools and Software

Chapter 4: Setting Up Operations

Chapter 5: Attracting Your First Clients

Chapter 6: Scaling for Growth

Chapter 7: Legal Compliance and Risk Management

Chapter 8: Managing Finances and Maximizing Profit

Chapter 9: Staying Ahead

Conclusion: Your Path to Success

Appendix

Copyright © 2024 Lamonee Coates

All rights reserved.

No part of this publication may be reproduced, distributed, or transmitted in any form or by any means, including photocopying, recording, or other electronic or mechanical methods, without the prior written permission of the publisher, except in the case of brief quotations embodied in critical reviews and certain other noncommercial uses permitted by copyright law.

Disclaimer: The information provided in this book is intended for educational and informational purposes only. While every effort has been made to ensure accuracy, the author and publisher assume no responsibility for errors, omissions, or any outcomes related to the application of this content. Readers are advised to consult professional advisors regarding their circumstances.

ISBN: 9798343828115
Published by: Lamonee Coates, Independently published
First Edition: October 2024

For permissions, inquiries, or bulk purchases, contact:
Lamoneec@gmail.com

INTRODUCTION

The tax industry presents an evergreen opportunity for entrepreneurs, with demand growing steadily as individuals and businesses require expert help to manage increasingly complex tax regulations. Launching a tax business in 2025 is more promising than ever, thanks to the rise of digital tools, remote services, and new industry niches like crypto taxation. Whether you're a seasoned accountant, an Enrolled Agent (EA), or a new entrepreneur looking for a stable business, the tax preparation field offers the potential for both flexibility and high profitability.

This guide provides a practical roadmap to help you navigate every step of launching a successful tax business—from legal setup and certifications to finding clients and scaling operations. We'll explore emerging trends, such as AI-powered tax tools and virtual consulting, giving you a competitive edge as the industry evolves. Following these steps, you'll learn to lay a solid foundation, attract your first clients, and build a thriving year-round business.

With tax laws constantly changing, proper knowledge and systems will set you apart. This book is designed to be your comprehensive toolkit—whether you aim to start small with individual clients or plan to scale into corporate tax consulting. Get ready to launch a business that provides financial independence and delivers essential value to your clients.

Chapter 1

Laying the Foundation

Starting a business is far from a risk-free venture, and success doesn't happen overnight. You shouldn't expect to make big profits immediately or only spend a couple of hours per week on it. Launching a business requires significant time, effort, and commitment, especially in the early stages. However, the rewards are well worth it. Every ounce of energy you invest directly benefits you, with all profits flowing into your pocket. Unlike a regular job, where income is capped, your business has the potential to grow exponentially—along with your profits. This exponential growth opens the door to financial freedom, offering an opportunity to break away from the constraints of a 9-to-5 lifestyle. Ultimately, building a successful business is one of the fastest paths to achieving financial independence and unlocking the potential for a six-figure income.

A tax business involves more than just knowing tax laws—you need a solid foundation to operate legally, attract clients, and manage your business effectively. This chapter will walk you through the initial setup steps, including selecting the proper business structure, registering your company, and securing essential licenses.

Choosing a Business Structure

Your business structure will impact how you're taxed, the paperwork you need, and your liability exposure. Common options include:

- **Sole Proprietorship:** Simple to set up, but you are personally liable for any debts or legal issues.
- **Limited Liability Company (LLC):** Offers personal liability protection with fewer regulations than a corporation.
- **S Corporation:** Provides tax advantages if you plan to scale your business.

Evaluate which structure aligns with your long-term goals. Consulting with a lawyer or accountant can help you make the best choice.

Registering Your Business and Obtaining Licenses

Once you decide on a structure, register your business with your state. You'll also need an Employer Identification Number (EIN) from the IRS if you plan to hire employees. Make sure to research local permits or licenses required to operate legally in your area.

Understanding the IRS Requirements (PTIN, EFIN)

To prepare taxes for compensation, you must apply for a Preparer Tax Identification Number (PTIN) through the IRS. If you intend to file returns electronically (which most clients prefer), you'll need an Electronic Filing Identification Number (EFIN). Both are free to obtain but require time to process, so apply early.

Setting Up a Business Bank Account and Insurance

Keep your business finances separate from personal ones by opening a dedicated business bank account. Consider obtaining Errors and Omissions (E&O) insurance to protect yourself from potential client disputes or mistakes during tax filing.

By carefully setting up these foundational elements, you'll avoid future headaches and establish a professional image that builds trust with clients.

Setting Up a Website for Your Business

In today's digital age, leveraging the Internet is essential for your business's success. Building a website establishes your online presence and opens the door to free, organic traffic over time. For instance, when potential clients search for "tax preparation" on Google and your site ranks among the results, you can attract a steady stream of visitors actively seeking your services. A well-crafted website also serves as a platform to showcase customer reviews, portfolios, your mission statement, and other key elements that help strengthen your brand over the long term. You can easily create a professional site using platforms like **WordPress** or **Wix**, or hire experts on **Fiverr** to design a high-quality website at an affordable price.

Chapter 2

Mastering the Tax Industry

The tax industry is dynamic, with new laws, technologies, and client demands shaping how businesses operate. To succeed in this new era, it's crucial to understand the industry's fundamentals and stay updated with evolving regulations. This chapter covers the basics of tax preparation, highlights essential certifications, and explores emerging niches that can set you apart from the competition.

Understanding Tax Preparation Basics

At its core, tax preparation involves helping individuals and businesses comply with federal, state, and local tax obligations. To offer valuable services, you must understand:

Personal Taxes: Forms like the 1040, deductions (e.g., mortgage interest, student loans), and credits (e.g., Earned Income Tax Credit).

Business Taxes: Corporate taxes, self-employment taxes, and payroll obligations for small businesses.

Quarterly Taxes: Estimated tax payments required for freelancers and companies.
Staying updated on filing deadlines and tax brackets ensures your clients avoid penalties and receive all eligible refunds.

Staying Updated on Tax Laws and Changes

Tax regulations change annually. New policies may affect areas like:

- **Crypto Taxes:** IRS regulations now require more transparency for cryptocurrency transactions.
- **Gig Economy Income:** Expanded rules for reporting freelance and contract work.
- **Energy Credits:** New incentives for green energy and electric vehicle purchases.

Use reliable sources like the IRS website, industry newsletters, and webinars to stay informed.

Important Certifications to Boost Your Credibility

Certifications can establish your expertise and help build trust with clients. Consider the following options:

- **Enrolled Agent (EA):** Certified by the IRS, EAs specialize in tax matters and represent clients before the IRS.
- **Certified Public Accountant (CPA):** A broader designation covering accounting, auditing, and taxes.
- **Annual Filing Season Program (AFSP):** An IRS-recognized certificate for non-credentialed preparers who want to demonstrate their knowledge.

Pursuing these certifications can enhance your marketability and allow you to charge higher fees.

Exploring the Profitable Niches

Specializing in a niche can help you stand out in a competitive market. Here are some trending areas:

- **Crypto Taxation:** Many taxpayers struggle to report cryptocurrency earnings correctly.
- **Freelancer and Gig Worker Taxes:** With the rise of remote work, gig economy workers need specialized tax help.
- **Small Business Compliance:** Offering payroll and sales tax services can attract business clients.
- **Green Tax Incentives:** Advising clients on energy-related credits and deductions can be a profitable niche.

Identifying a niche that aligns with your expertise and market demand can give your business a competitive edge.

Leveraging Technology for Efficiency

Technology plays a crucial role in modern tax businesses. Staying competitive requires investing in the right tools:

- **Tax Preparation Software:** Solutions like TurboTax, Drake, and Lacerte help you prepare accurate returns efficiently.
- **AI and Automation Tools:** Automate repetitive tasks like data entry and filing to save time.
- **Client Portals:** Secure platforms for uploading documents and communicating with clients remotely.

- **eSignature Tools:** Tools like DocuSign simplify the signing process and provide legal compliance.

Integrating AI and automation tools into your tax business can significantly boost efficiency, accuracy, and client satisfaction. Software like **Lacerte** and **ProConnect Tax Online** automate complex calculations, e-filing, and error-checking, reducing manual workloads. Tools such as **Dext** leverage AI-powered OCR to extract data from receipts and invoices, streamlining deduction tracking and document management.

For enhanced compliance, platforms like **Avalara** and **Thomson Reuters ONESOURCE** automatically update tax codes and generate real-time reports, minimizing the risk of audits. Lastly, **Zapier** and **HubSpot** automate workflows by connecting tax software with CRM systems, simplifying client onboarding, follow-ups, and appointment scheduling.

Utilizing the latest technology allows you to focus on advisory service while automation handles repetitive tasks, ensuring accuracy, compliance, and timely service delivery.

Participating in online forums, webinars, and continuing education courses is another key to help you stay ahead of industry trends and maintain your credentials.

The tax industry rewards professionals who commit to lifelong learning. Join organizations like the **National Association of Enrolled Agents (NAEA)** or the **American Institute of CPAs (AICPA)** to stay connected with peers, attend industry events, and access exclusive resources.

By mastering the tax industry's core concepts, regulations, and technologies, you'll be well-prepared to serve your clients confidently.

Chapter 3

Essential Tools and Software

Running a successful tax business requires more than just knowledge of tax laws—you'll need the right tools to streamline operations, manage clients, and ensure compliance. Explore the critical software solutions and technology platforms needed to build a smooth, scalable business. Adopting the right tech stack, from tax preparation software to communication tools, will save you time, reduce errors, and enhance client satisfaction.

Choosing the Right Tax Preparation Software

Reliable tax preparation software is the backbone of your business. It automates calculations, helps you file accurately, and ensures compliance with changing tax regulations. Some popular options are:

- **TurboTax Business:** Best for smaller tax practices handling individual and small business returns.
- **Drake Tax:** Offers comprehensive features with flexible pricing, ideal for businesses with multiple preparers.
- **Lacerte Tax:** Provides robust tools for handling complex tax filings, including corporate and partnership returns.

When selecting software, consider the types of clients you'll serve, the user interface, and available support. Most platforms also offer free trials, so exploring a few is necessary before committing.

Accounting and Bookkeeping Tools

To manage your finances effectively, you'll need tools that help track revenue, expenses, and payroll. Some popular options include

- **QuickBooks Online:** Perfect for tracking expenses, generating invoices, and managing payroll.
- **Xero:** A cloud-based alternative with strong reporting features and integration options.
- **Wave Accounting:** Free software designed for freelancers and small businesses.

These tools also simplify bookkeeping services if you plan to offer them as an additional

Client Management and Communication Platforms

Managing multiple clients and ensuring seamless communication is essential for success. A **CRM (Customer Relationship Management)** tool can help organize client details. Consider these options:

- **HubSpot CRM:** A free platform for tracking interactions, storing documents, and managing leads.

- **TaxDome:** Specifically designed for tax firms, offering a client portal, CRM features, and workflow automation.

Use these tools to manage deadlines, follow-ups, and secure document exchanges, creating a professional experience for your clients.

Document Management and Security Tools

Handling sensitive client data comes with responsibilities. Implementing secure storage and document management tools is crucial:

- **Google Drive or Dropbox:** Cloud-based platforms with encryption to store and share documents.
- **SmartVault:** A more specialized document storage solution tailored for tax professionals.
- **eSignature Tools:** Use platforms like DocuSign or Adobe Sign to collect legally compliant signatures remotely.

Storing data securely protects your clients and ensures your compliance with data privacy laws.

AI and Automation for Workflow Efficiency

Incorporating **AI-powered tools** can help automate routine tasks and improve accuracy. For example:

- **Canopy Tax:** Automates client onboarding, invoicing, and communications.

- **Zapier:** Connects apps and automates workflows, like sending reminders for unpaid invoices.
- **ChatGPT or similar AI assistants:** Use AI tools to answer routine client inquiries or generate content for your website.

Tax Compliance Tools and IRS Portals

Ensure your practice stays compliant by regularly using essential IRS tools and portals:

- **IRS e-Services Portal:** For submitting forms and checking client information.
- **Tax Compliance Monitoring Software:** Tools like Avalara help track changes in tax laws and ensure accurate filings.

Staying proactive with compliance reduces the risk of audits and builds trust with clients.

Video Conferencing and Remote Work Tools

With remote tax services becoming the norm, you'll need reliable tools for virtual consultations:

- **Zoom or Microsoft Teams:** For virtual meetings and screen sharing.
- **Calendly:** Automates scheduling and integrates with your calendar to reduce back-and-forth emails.

A seamless remote experience will help you reach clients across different regions and maintain flexibility in your work environment.

Building a Website and Online Presence

A professional website is essential for attracting new clients. Platforms like **Squarespace** and **Wix** offer easy-to-use templates, while **WordPress** provides more customization options. Make sure your website includes:

- A description of your services
- Pricing information
- A client portal for uploading documents securely
- Contact information and scheduling options.

Optimizing your site for **SEO (Search Engine Optimization)** will also help attract clients organically through Google searches.

Streamlining Your Business with the Right Tools

Equipping your tax business with the right tools and software will allow you to manage clients efficiently, ensure compliance, and streamline workflows. From tax preparation software and accounting tools to AI-powered automation and secure communication platforms, each tool you adopt brings you closer to building a scalable, profitable business.

Chapter 4
Setting Up Operations

Once your tax business is legally registered and equipped with the right tools, the next step is to set up efficient operations. Proper workflows, an organized workspace, and effective processes are essential for smooth daily activities. In this chapter, we'll cover how to design an ideal workspace, develop workflows, manage remote versus in-person services, and determine pricing for profitability.

Creating Workflows for Tax Preparation

An effective workflow is the backbone of any tax business. It streamlines how you handle client intake, prepare tax returns, and communicate with clients. Here's a step-by-step breakdown of a typical tax workflow:

1. **Client Onboarding:**

Collect client information using a secure form or client portal.
Use a checklist to gather the necessary documents (W-2s, 1099s, etc.).
Set expectations by outlining your process and timeline.

2. **Document Review:**

Review documents for completeness and accuracy. Use tax software to import and organize client data.

3. **Tax Return Preparation:**

Input data into your tax preparation software.

Double-check calculations and deductions using built-in review tools.

4. **Client Review:**

Schedule a meeting (virtual or in-person) to review the return.

Use e-signature tools to get approval for filing.

5. **Filing and Follow-up:**

File electronically and confirm receipt with the IRS or state.

Send a follow-up email with the final return, payment details, and a thank-you message.

This workflow ensures that nothing falls through the cracks, and it provides a clear, repeatable process that saves time and reduces stress.

Setting Up an Office:
Home-Based vs. Commercial Space

Deciding where to operate your tax business depends on your budget, business model, and client needs. Here are the pros and cons of each option:

Home-Based Office
- Pros:

Lower overhead costs.
Flexibility and convenience.
Tax deductions for home office expenses.
- **Cons:**

May appear less professional to certain clients.
Potential distractions.
Limited space for in-person client meetings.

Commercial Office Space
- **Pros:**

Professional appearance, which can build client trust.
Room to meet clients and employees in person.
It may be necessary if you plan to scale your business.
- **Cons:**

Higher rent and operational costs.
Long-term lease commitments may reduce flexibility.

For many new tax professionals, starting with a home-based office is an innovative and cost-effective choice. However, if you expect high foot traffic or plan to grow quickly, investing in a small office may offer a more professional image.

Remote vs. In-Person Services: Pros and Cons

The ability to offer remote services has become essential. Here's a look at both models:

Remote Services

- **Pros:**

Broader client base (you can serve clients nationwide).
Lower overhead costs.
Convenience for clients and flexibility for you.

- **Cons:**

Lack of personal interaction, can hinder relationship-building.
Requires reliable technology and secure communication tools.

In-Person Services

- **Pros:**

Builds stronger personal relationships with clients.
Easier to explain complex tax issues face-to-face.

- **Cons:**

Limits your client base to a specific geographic area.
Higher costs for maintaining an office and meeting space.

Most tax businesses today combine both models, offering in-person consultations for local clients while handling the majority of tax filings remotely.

Pricing Your Services: Hourly vs. Flat Fees

Setting the right pricing structure is key to attracting clients while ensuring profitability. There are two main models: hourly rates and flat fees.

Hourly Rates

- **Pros:**

Transparent and easy to explain to clients.
It is better for complex cases that require more time.

- **Cons:**

Clients may be reluctant if they perceive they are being charged for too much time.

It is harder to predict income, especially during the busy season.

Flat Fees

- **Pros:**

Predictable income for both you and your clients.
More straightforward when selling to clients because they know the total cost upfront.

- **Cons:**

If a case is more complicated than expected, you may lose time or money.
It requires more planning to ensure your fee structure covers your operating costs.

Many tax preparers use a hybrid pricing model, charging flat fees for standard services (like individual returns) and hourly rates for more complex cases (like business tax filings or audits).

Scheduling and Managing Your Time

Tax season can be overwhelming without a solid time management strategy. Consider these tips for maximizing efficiency:

- **Batch Similar Tasks:** Dedicate specific time slots for reviewing documents, preparing returns, and client communication.
- **Use Scheduling Tools:** Platforms like Calendly or Acuity allow clients to book appointments automatically, reducing back-and-forth communication.
- **Set Boundaries:** Clearly define your office hours to avoid burnout and ensure clients know when to expect responses.

Efficient scheduling will allow you to take on more clients while maintaining high service quality.

Building a Professional Image

A well-organized business operation creates a professional image that attracts clients and builds trust. Here's how to enhance that image:

- **Use Branded Documents:** Create templates with your logo and professional design for proposals, invoices, and reports.

- **Establish a Client Portal:** Offer clients a secure way to upload documents and view their progress.
- **Maintain a Professional Website:** Ensure your website is easy to navigate and provides a clear overview of your services, pricing, and contact information.

The goal is to offer a seamless, polished experience for your clients, from their first inquiry to the final tax filing.

Laying the Groundwork for Success

Setting up efficient operations involves careful planning, streamlined workflows, and the right business model for your needs.

Whether you choose to work from home or a commercial office, offer remote or in-person services, or charge hourly or flat fees, the key is to create a system that works for you and your clients. With a solid operational setup, you'll be well-prepared to manage your workload, serve clients effectively, and grow your tax business over time.

Chapter 5
Attracting Your First Clients

Once your business is up and running, your next priority should be attracting clients. It's unlikely that potential customers will find you on their own, especially in the beginning. Therefore, you'll need to take a proactive approach to secure your first clients and start building momentum.

Winning your first client is pivotal in launching a successful tax business. Your initial clients will generate revenue and help build your reputation through referrals and testimonials.

Define Your Target Audience

To attract clients, it's essential to understand who they are and what they need. Start by identifying specific groups you want to serve:

- **Individuals:** Young professionals, retirees, or people with unique tax situations (e.g., homeowners, students).
- **Small Business Owners:** Entrepreneurs, freelancers, and gig workers with complex tax needs.
- **Specialized Niches:** Clients with crypto investments, rental properties, or green energy incentives.

Defining your niche allows you to tailor your services and marketing efforts to attract the right clients.

Create a Professional Brand and Online Presence

First impressions matter. A well-designed brand makes your business more trustworthy and appealing to potential clients. Here's how to build your brand:

- **Create a Logo:** Use tools like Canva or hire a designer to create a professional logo that reflects your business values.
- **Business Cards:** Business cards are a valuable tool in the tax preparation industry, as nearly everyone needs to file taxes. Handing out well-designed cards helps you connect with potential clients effortlessly. Ensure your card is visually appealing and includes your contact details, making it easy for prospects to contact you when they need your services.
- **Optimize for SEO:** Use keywords like "tax preparation services near me" or "freelancer tax filing" to help clients find you through Google searches.
- **Claim Your Business Listings:** Set up profiles on Google My Business, Yelp, and other local directories to increase visibility.

A strong online presence helps establish your credibility and makes it easy for potential clients to find and contact you.

Leverage Word-of-Mouth and Referrals

Referrals are one of the most powerful ways to attract new clients. Here's how to encourage them:

- **Offer Referral Incentives:** Provide discounts or small bonuses to clients who refer new business to you.
- **Ask for Testimonials:** Collect reviews from satisfied clients and showcase them on your website and social media.
- **Network with Local Professionals:** Build relationships with other business owners, such as financial advisors, real estate agents, or lawyers, who can refer clients to you.

A happy client base can become your most effective marketing tool.

Social Media Marketing and Networking

Establishing a social media presence is essential in today's digital landscape, where social platforms dominate. Create accounts for your business and focus on sharing engaging, relevant content that resonates with your target audience. As your following grows over time, many of these connections are likely to convert into paying clients. While this approach requires consistent effort, it's a long-term strategy that can deliver significant returns on your investment of time and help sustain your business's growth.

- **Facebook and Instagram:** Share tax tips, deadline reminders, and client success stories. Use targeted ads to reach local clients.
- **LinkedIn:** Position yourself as a tax expert by sharing articles, participating in discussions, and networking with other professionals.
- **YouTube or TikTok:** Create videos explaining common tax issues, such as how to file crypto taxes or maximize deductions.

Consistent engagement helps build trust and keeps your business in mind when clients need tax services.

Offer Free Resources or Workshops

Providing free value is a great way to attract clients and demonstrate your expertise. Here are a few ideas.

- **Free Tax Consultations:** Offer a 15- to 30-minute consultation to answer client questions and introduce your services.
- **Workshops or Webinars:** Host an event on common tax topics (e.g., "Maximize Your Deductions for 2025") to position yourself as an expert.
- **Downloadable Guides:** Create a free ebook or checklist (e.g., "Top 10 Tax Deductions for Freelancers") that visitors can download from your website.

These strategies provide value upfront, helping you build relationships and convert leads into paying clients.

Networking Events and Local Partnerships

Building relationships with local businesses and organizations can help grow your client base.

- **Attend Networking Events:** Join business associations, chamber of commerce events, or professional meetups to connect with potential clients.
- **Partner with Local Businesses:** Offer co-branded promotions or workshops with businesses that share your audience (e.g., accounting firms or coworking spaces).
- **Sponsor Community Events:** Supporting a local event can increase your visibility and demonstrate your commitment to the community.

Networking helps you establish trust and opens doors to new client opportunities.

Offer Seasonal Promotions and Discounts

Seasonal promotions can create urgency and attract new clients during peak filing periods. Consider these strategies:

- **Early-Bird Discounts:** Offer discounts for clients who file early in the season.
- **Loyalty Programs:** Provide discounts or rewards for repeat clients who use your services yearly.
- **Holiday Promotions:** Use holidays like New Year's or tax season kickoff events to offer limited-time promotions.

These incentives encourage clients to act quickly and create momentum for your business.

Use Paid Advertising for Faster Growth

If you want to attract clients quickly, paid advertising can be a powerful tool.

- **Google Ads:** Use search ads targeting keywords like "tax preparer near me" or "business tax filing services."
- **Facebook Ads:** Target specific demographics or interests relevant to your services (e.g., freelancers, small business owners).
- **Direct Mail Campaigns:** Send postcards or flyers to local residents and businesses promoting your tax services.

Paid advertising, when done strategically, can generate leads quickly and boost brand awareness.

Provide Exceptional Service to Retain Clients

Attracting clients is only half the battle—retaining them is just as important. Here's how to ensure clients return year after year:

- **Personalized Service:** Get to know your clients and tailor your advice to their specific tax situation.
- **Proactive Communication:** Send reminders about deadlines, new tax laws, or opportunities for additional savings.

- **Follow-Up and Appreciation:** After filing, follow up with clients to ensure they're satisfied. Send thank-you notes or small gifts to show appreciation for their business.

Satisfied clients are more likely to return and refer others, providing you with a steady stream of business.

Building a Strong Client Base

Attracting your first clients requires a combination of targeted marketing, professional branding, and exceptional service. By defining your niche, building a strong online presence, leveraging referrals, and networking effectively, you'll position your tax business for steady growth. Offering free resources, seasonal promotions, and paid ads can further boost your efforts. Once you've attracted clients, providing personalized service and building long-term relationships will ensure they stay with you year after year.

Chapter 6
Scaling for Growth

Once your tax business has a solid foundation and a steady stream of clients, it's time to focus on scaling for growth. Scaling is more than just adding clients—it requires strategic planning to ensure your business grows sustainably while maintaining quality. This chapter explores essential strategies for hiring, automating processes, expanding your services, and building long-term growth.

Expanding Your Service Offerings

One way to grow your business is by increasing the range of services you offer. This allows you to attract new clients and increase revenue from existing ones. Here are some ideas for complementary services:

- **Bookkeeping and Accounting Services:** Offer year-round bookkeeping to small businesses and freelancers.
- **Payroll Services:** Provide payroll management for small business clients.
- **Tax Resolution Services:** Help clients navigate audits, disputes, or back taxes with the IRS.
- **Financial Consulting:** Advise clients on tax planning, retirement strategies, or wealth management.

Adding new services creates multiple revenue streams and builds deeper relationships with your clients.

Hiring and Building a Team

As your business grows, you'll likely need help managing the workload. Hiring the right team allows you to delegate tasks and focus on strategic growth. Here are key roles to consider:

- **Administrative Assistants:** Handle scheduling, client communication, and document management.
- **Tax Preparers:** Assist with tax filings, freeing you to focus on complex cases or client management.
- **Bookkeepers:** Manage bookkeeping and payroll services for your business clients.
- **Marketing Specialists:** Help with social media, email campaigns, and other marketing activities.

As your business grows, you'll need to hire additional staff to manage operations, making effective training essential for maintaining high-quality service. Start by enrolling new hires in a basic tax preparation course and guiding them through the process of obtaining a PTIN. It's equally important to introduce them to your company's privacy policies. For example, many financial institutions require employees handling sensitive client information to lock their devices when not in use to prevent data breaches. Implementing similar protocols will reassure clients that their data is secure.

Ideally, you'll only need to train the first few employees you hire personally. As your team expands, these trained staff members can take over the onboarding and training of future hires. This creates a continuous cycle where the knowledge and standards you establish are passed down throughout your workforce. Therefore, taking the initial training seriously is crucial, as it will shape your company's culture, service quality, and long-term success.

Whether you hire part-time, full-time, or freelance employees, clear job descriptions and training are essential to ensure consistency in service quality.

Automation and Workflow Optimization

Automation is critical to scaling your tax business. It reduces manual work, improves efficiency, and ensures consistent service delivery. Consider automating the following areas:

- **Client Onboarding:** Use automated forms and client portals to collect information and documents.
- **Appointment Scheduling:** Tools like Calendly can streamline meeting bookings and reduce back-and-forth emails.
- **Invoicing and Payments:** Automate invoices, payment reminders, and receipts using accounting software like QuickBooks.
- **Marketing Campaigns:** Set up automated email campaigns to nurture leads and retain clients

Outsourcing Non-Core Tasks

To stay focused on your core services, consider outsourcing tasks that are outside your expertise or take up too much time. Examples include:

- **Marketing and Social Media Management:** Hire a specialist or agency to manage your online presence.
- **IT Support:** Use an external service to handle tech issues, data security, and software management.
- **Legal and Compliance:** Outsource legal tasks like contracts and business registrations to ensure compliance with regulations.

Strategic outsourcing helps you stay lean and efficient while tapping into specialized expertise.

Implementing Systems for Client Retention and Referrals

Scaling your business isn't just about attracting new clients—it's also about retaining the ones you have. Satisfied clients are more likely to return and refer others. Here are strategies for client retention:

- **Loyalty Programs:** Offer discounts or perks to repeat clients who return each year.
- **Follow-Up Communication:** Stay in touch with clients throughout the year by sending tax tips, reminders, and relevant updates.
- **Referral Programs:** Reward clients who refer friends or colleagues with discounts or small gifts.

Building long-term relationships with your clients ensures sustainable growth through word-of-mouth marketing.

Monitoring Business Metrics and Performance

Tracking key metrics helps you make data-driven decisions and ensures your business is on the right growth path. Here are some key performance indicators (KPIs) to monitor:

- **Revenue Growth:** Track how much your revenue increases each quarter or year.
- **Client Retention Rate:** Measure the percentage of clients who return each year.
- **Average Revenue per Client:** Assess how much value each client brings to your business.
- **Profit Margin:** Ensure that your expenses are under control and you're maintaining healthy profits.

Regularly reviewing these metrics helps you identify opportunities and challenges so you can adjust your strategy accordingly.

Exploring New Markets and Niches

If your local market is becoming saturated, consider expanding your reach by targeting new niches or regions. Some ideas include:

- **Online and Remote Services:** Expand beyond your local area by offering fully remote services to clients nationwide.
- **Specialized Niches:** Position yourself as an expert in areas like cryptocurrency taxation or nonprofit tax filings.
- **Franchising or Partnerships:** Collaborate with other professionals or explore the possibility of franchising your business model.

Expanding your market helps you diversify your client base and open new growth opportunities.

Staying Updated with Tax Laws and Industry Trends

As the tax industry evolves, staying up-to-date with tax laws, regulations, and software changes is essential for scaling your business. Here's how to stay informed:

- **Continuing Education:** Enroll in courses and certifications to sharpen your expertise and meet IRS requirements.
- **Industry Conferences:** Attend conferences and networking events to learn about emerging trends and tools.
- **Professional Memberships:** Join industry organizations like the National Association of Tax Professionals (NATP) to stay connected and informed.

Staying current ensures you're always offering clients the most accurate advice and solutions.

Financing Growth and Managing Cash Flow

Scaling often requires investment—whether for hiring staff, upgrading software, or expanding your office space. Managing cash flow is crucial to ensure you can fund growth without jeopardizing your business.

Consider these options:

- **Business Loans or Credit Lines:** Use financing to cover expansion costs.
- **Profit Reinvestment:** Reinvest profits into hiring, marketing, or technology upgrades.
- **Expense Management:** Keep track of expenses to ensure profitability and avoid cash flow issues during slow seasons.

A clear financial strategy ensures you can scale sustainably without overextending your resources.

Building a Scalable, Sustainable Business

Scaling your tax business requires thoughtful planning, efficient systems, and a focus on growth and client satisfaction. By expanding your service offerings, hiring the right team, automating workflows, and monitoring key metrics, you'll create a business that grows sustainably. Exploring new markets, staying current with industry trends, and managing cash flow effectively will further position your business for long-term success.

Chapter 7
Legal Compliance and Risk Management

Running a tax business requires more than just filing returns and providing advice—it involves navigating a complex landscape of legal and regulatory requirements. Ensuring compliance and managing risks is essential to protecting your business, maintaining your clients' trust, and avoiding costly penalties. In this chapter, we'll cover the key legal obligations, how to reduce liability, and the importance of data security and ethical practices.

Registering Your Business and Meeting Licensing Requirements

Before offering tax services, ensure your business complies with federal, state, and local regulations.

- **Business Registration:** Choose a legal structure (LLC, S-Corp, or sole proprietorship) and register with your state.
- **EIN (Employer Identification Number):** Obtain an EIN from the IRS if you hire employees or operate as an LLC or corporation.

- **State Licensing**: Some states require tax preparers to obtain specific licenses or registrations. Check your state's regulations to ensure compliance.
- **IRS PTIN (Preparer Tax Identification Number)**: Anyone preparing tax returns for compensation must register for a PTIN with the IRS.

Meeting these requirements establishes your business's legitimacy and avoids penalties for non-compliance.

Adhering to IRS and State Regulations

The IRS and individual states have strict rules for tax preparers. Ensure you meet the following standards:

- **Annual Filing Season Program (AFSP)**: Completing AFSP certification enhances your credibility and gives you limited representation rights before the IRS.
- **Continuing Education (CE)**: Stay current with IRS-required education to remain compliant and provide accurate advice.
- **Ethical Practices**: Follow IRS guidelines for ethical behavior outlined in Circular 230, which governs tax professionals.

Failure to comply with these standards can result in fines, suspension of licenses, or even legal action.

Managing Legal Risks and Liability

Like any business, a tax practice carries risks. These can range from human errors to IRS audits and client disputes. Here are strategies to minimize risks:

- **Errors and Omissions Insurance (E&O):** This insurance protects your business from negligence claims or mistakes in tax filings.
- **Client Engagement Letters:** Use detailed engagement letters to outline the scope of your services, fees, and limitations. This ensures clarity and sets expectations upfront.
- **Audit Protection Plans:** Consider offering audit support as an optional service to help clients in the event of an IRS audit.

Managing liability proactively helps protect your business and builds client trust.

Safeguarding Client Data and Ensuring Data Privacy

Handling sensitive financial information comes with significant responsibility. Ensuring data security is not just a best practice—it's a legal obligation.

- **Use Encrypted Software:** Store client data in secure, encrypted databases to protect against data breaches.
- **Secure Communication:** Use secure email systems or client portals to exchange sensitive information

- **Compliance with IRS Data Security Requirements:** The IRS mandates specific security practices for tax professionals, such as multi-factor authentication (MFA) and regular software updates.
- **Shred Physical Documents:** Destroy printed materials containing personal information to prevent unauthorized access.

Data breaches can result in legal penalties, reputational damage, and loss of clients. Prioritize security to safeguard both your clients and your business.

Understanding and Managing Tax Preparer Penalties

The IRS imposes penalties on tax professionals for errors, misconduct, or non-compliance. Familiarize yourself with the most common penalties:

- **Accuracy-Related Penalties:** Applied if the IRS finds substantial errors in filed returns.
- **Failure-to-File Penalties:** Charged if returns are filed late or not at all.
- **Preparer Penalty for Willful or Reckless Conduct:** A steep penalty for knowingly preparing false or fraudulent returns.

Avoid penalties by implementing thorough review processes, continuing education, and adherence to IRS guidelines.

Handling Client Disputes and Legal Issues

Despite your best efforts, disputes with clients may arise. Here's how to handle them professionally:

- **Maintain Clear Documentation:** Keep records of all communications, agreements, and transactions with clients.
- **Resolve Issues Quickly:** Address client concerns promptly and offer solutions, such as corrections or refunds, if appropriate.
- **Mediation and Arbitration:** Include dispute resolution clauses in engagement letters to outline how conflicts will be handled outside of court.

Managing disputes calmly and transparently protects your reputation and prevents escalation into legal battles.

Compliance with Employment Laws and Contractor Agreements

If you plan to hire employees or work with contractors, it's essential to comply with employment laws.

- **Employment Contracts:** Clearly define job roles, compensation, and responsibilities to avoid misunderstandings.
- **Worker Classification:** Ensure contractors and employees are classified correctly to avoid IRS penalties.
- **Payroll Taxes and Benefits:** Comply with federal and state regulations for employee benefits and payroll taxes.

Managing these legal obligations ensures smooth operations and avoids fines or legal complications.

The Importance of Ethical Practices

Maintaining high ethical standards is key to building a sustainable tax business. Ethics go beyond legal requirements and influence your reputation and relationships. Follow these principles:

- **Transparency:** Be clear about your fees, processes, and potential risks.
- **Confidentiality:** Respect your clients' privacy and never share information without consent.
- **Integrity:** Always act in your clients' best interests, even if it means referring them elsewhere.

Ethical behavior builds trust and helps you stand out in a competitive industry.

Staying Updated on Changing Regulations

The tax landscape changes frequently, with new laws, policies, and compliance requirements emerging each year. Here's how to stay up-to-date:

- **IRS and State Websites:** Monitor official websites for updates and announcements.
- **Industry Newsletters and Publications:** Subscribe to newsletters from reputable organizations like the IRS, NATP, or AICPA.

- **Continuing Education Courses:** Attend courses and webinars to stay current on tax law changes and best practices.

Keeping your knowledge current ensures your business remains compliant and competitive.

Building a Legally Compliant and Risk-Proof Business

Legal compliance and risk management are essential to protecting your tax business and maintaining trust with your clients. By following IRS and state regulations, securing client data, and managing liability through insurance and contracts, you'll create a solid legal framework for your business. Handling disputes professionally, maintaining ethical standards, and staying current with changes in the industry will position your business for long-term success.

Chapter 8

Managing Finances and Maximizing Profit

Effective financial management is the backbone of a profitable tax business. Beyond generating revenue, you must ensure healthy cash flow, control expenses, and plan for the future. In this chapter, we'll explore strategies for budgeting, tracking expenses, managing taxes, and optimizing profitability to build a sustainable, growth-ready business.

Budgeting for Success

Creating a realistic budget is the first step in managing your business's finances. A well-planned budget helps you allocate resources effectively and prevents overspending.

Review your budget regularly to make adjustments and stay on track.

- **Fixed Expenses:** Include rent, software subscriptions, utilities, and payroll costs.
- **Variable Expenses:** Factor in marketing costs, supplies, and professional development expenses.

- **Emergency Fund:** Set aside cash for unexpected expenses like equipment repairs or legal fees.
- **Seasonality:** Consider the seasonal nature of tax preparation and plan for slow months.

Tracking Income and Expenses

Accurate bookkeeping ensures a clear picture of your financial health and simplifies tax filing. Use these practices to stay organized:

- **Accounting Software:** Use software like QuickBooks or Xero to automate bookkeeping and track income and expenses.
- **Separate Business Accounts:** Maintain separate bank accounts and credit cards for your business to avoid personal expense confusion.
- **Weekly or Monthly Reconciliation:** Regularly match your financial records with bank statements to catch discrepancies early.
- **Expense Categories:** Organize expenses into categories like rent, payroll, marketing, and software for better analysis.

Clear records help you make informed financial decisions and prepare for audits if necessary.

Cash Flow Management

Cash flow refers to the movement of money in and out of your business. Poor cash flow management is one of the main reasons small businesses fail, so staying on top of it is essential.

- **Monitor Receivables:** Set clear payment terms and send invoices promptly to avoid delays.
- **Manage Payables:** Negotiate longer payment terms with vendors to improve cash flow.
- **Forecast Cash Flow:** Use historical data to predict future cash flow, especially for slow seasons.
- **Maintain a Buffer:** Keep a cash reserve to handle unexpected expenses and cover payroll during off-peak periods.

Positive cash flow ensures your business can meet its financial obligations without stress.

Managing Taxes and Compliance

As a tax professional, you're expected to practice what you preach. Staying on top of your own business taxes is crucial to maintaining credibility and avoiding penalties.

- **Estimated Quarterly Taxes:** Calculate and pay estimated taxes to avoid underpayment penalties.
- **Business Deductions:** Track deductible expenses such as office rent, software fees, and marketing costs to reduce your taxable income.

- **Sales Tax Compliance:** If you sell products or services that require sales tax, ensure you register with the appropriate tax authorities and file returns on time.
- **Payroll Taxes:** Stay compliant with payroll tax regulations if you have employees or independent contractors.

A well-organized tax strategy saves money and keeps your business compliant.

Controlling Costs and Reducing Overhead

Profitability is not just about earning more revenue—it's also about managing expenses. Here are ways to reduce costs and increase profitability:

- **Evaluate Subscriptions:** Review software and service subscriptions to eliminate those you no longer need.
- **Negotiate with Vendors:** Ask for discounts or explore alternative vendors to lower costs.
- **Outsource Select Functions:** Use freelancers or contractors for non-core tasks to reduce payroll expenses.
- **Go Paperless:** Minimize office supply costs by digitizing records and using cloud storage.

By keeping your overhead low, you'll improve your profit margins and reinvest more into your business.

Pricing Your Services for Profit

Setting the right pricing strategy is critical to maintaining profitability while staying competitive. Here are some pricing strategies to consider:

- **Flat-Fee Pricing:** Charge a set fee for specific services, such as personal or business tax returns.
- **Hourly Rates:** Use hourly billing for consulting or advisory services.
- **Tiered Pricing:** Offer different service levels with varying prices to accommodate clients with different budgets.
- **Value-Based Pricing:** Price your services based on the value you provide, rather than just the time spent.

Regularly evaluate your pricing and adjust as needed to reflect industry trends and your experience level.

Maximizing Profitability through Upselling and Cross-Selling

Upselling and cross-selling to existing clients is an effective way to boost revenue without increasing your marketing spend.

- **Offer Tax Planning Services:** Sell year-round tax planning to help clients minimize their future tax liabilities.
- **Cross-Sell Bookkeeping Services:** Provide bookkeeping services to business clients during off-peak tax seasons.

- **Audit Support Packages:** Offer clients audit protection plans for additional peace of mind.
- **Bundle Services:** Create service packages that combine multiple offerings at a discounted rate.

These strategies increase your revenue per client and create long-term relationships.

Measuring Key Financial Metrics

Tracking financial performance helps you identify areas for improvement and make data-driven decisions. Key metrics to monitor include:

- **Profit Margin:** Measure the percentage of revenue that turns into profit after expenses.
- **Client Acquisition Cost (CAC):** Calculate how much you spend on marketing to acquire each new client.
- **Lifetime Value (LTV) of a Client:** Assess how much revenue a client generates over the duration of your relationship.
- **Revenue per Employee:** If you have a team, measure the amount of revenue generated per employee.

Regular financial analysis keeps your business on track and helps you spot potential issues early.

Planning for Growth and Investments

Managing profits isn't just about the present—it's also about planning for future growth. Here's how to ensure sustainable growth:

- **Reinvest Profits:** Allocate a portion of profits toward marketing, technology upgrades, and employee development.
- **Apply for Business Credit:** Build business credit to secure financing for future expansion when needed.
- **Create a Retirement Plan:** Set up a retirement plan, such as a solo 401(k) or SEP IRA, to secure your financial future.
- **Prepare for Economic Changes:** Maintain a financial buffer to weather market downturns or economic slowdowns.

Smart investments ensure your business can scale and thrive in the long run.

Creating a Financially Sustainable Business

Managing your finances effectively is essential to maximizing profit and ensuring long-term success. By creating a realistic budget, monitoring cash flow, controlling expenses, and pricing services strategically, you'll set your business on a path to profitability. Staying organized with bookkeeping, managing your own taxes, and planning for future investments will ensure financial stability as you grow.

Chapter 9

Staying Ahead

The tax industry is evolving faster than ever, driven by changing regulations, technological advancements, and shifting client expectations. To remain competitive, you must continually adapt, improve, and stay ahead of industry trends. In this final chapter, we'll explore how to future-proof your business and position yourself as a leader in the tax industry now and beyond.

Embrace Industry Trends and Technology

Staying on top of trends ensures that your business remains relevant and offers value to clients. Key developments to monitor include:

- **AI and Automation:** Use AI-powered tools to streamline tasks like data entry, client communication, and financial analysis. Automation reduces errors and allows you to focus on higher-value services.
- **Blockchain and Tax Solutions:** Blockchain technology may influence how financial records are managed, offering more secure, tamper-proof transaction histories.
- **Real-Time Tax Reporting:** Governments are moving toward real-time tax submission models. Be prepared to adopt tools that can integrate with these systems.

- **Green Tax Credits and ESG Reporting:** With the rise of sustainability initiatives, clients may seek advice on green tax incentives and ESG (Environmental, Social, and Governance) reporting.

Being an early adopter of technology allows you to provide cutting-edge solutions and build a reputation as an innovative firm.

Expand Your Expertise with Continuing Education

Tax laws and regulations change frequently, requiring constant learning to maintain accuracy and compliance.

- **Specialize in Niche Markets:** Develop expertise in areas like cryptocurrency taxation, international tax, or small business consulting to attract new client segments.
- **Stay Certified:** Complete IRS-required continuing education annually to maintain compliance and earn credentials that set you apart.
- **Join Professional Organizations:** Participate in groups like the National Association of Tax Professionals (NATP) to stay connected with industry developments and attend networking events.

Continuous learning will give you a competitive edge and inspire confidence in your clients.

Build a Resilient and Agile Business Model

The ability to pivot quickly in response to external changes—whether market fluctuations, new regulations, or client needs—will be key to long-term success.

- **Develop Virtual Service Options:** Continue offering remote tax consultations and digital client portals to accommodate clients who prefer online services.
- **Diversify Your Revenue Streams:** Offer complementary services like financial planning, bookkeeping, or business consulting to reduce dependence on seasonal income.
- **Use Flexible Staffing Models:** Employ a mix of full-time staff, part-time employees, and independent contractors to scale operations up or down as needed.
- **Scenario Planning:** Develop contingency plans for economic downturns or changes in tax law that could affect your business.

Resilience will help you thrive no matter what challenges arise.

Enhance Client Experience with Personalization

Client expectations are evolving, with a growing focus on personalized service and proactive advice. Here's how to stay ahead of the curve:

- **Tailor Communication:** Use CRM (Customer Relationship Management) tools to personalize emails, reminders, and follow-ups for each client.

- **Proactive Tax Planning:** Offer clients year-round planning sessions to help them prepare for tax obligations and reduce liabilities.
- **Build Trust Through Transparency:** Be upfront about your fees, processes, and expected outcomes to build long-term client relationships.
- **Leverage Client Feedback:** Use surveys and feedback tools to understand client needs and improve your services continually.

Invest in Brand Building and Marketing

Creating a strong brand and digital presence will help you attract clients in an increasingly competitive marketplace.

- **Thought Leadership:** Publish articles, blog posts, or eBooks on emerging tax topics to establish yourself as a thought leader.
- **Leverage Social Media:** Engage with potential clients on platforms like LinkedIn and Instagram by sharing relevant content and industry insights.
- **Develop a Referral Program:** Encourage satisfied clients to refer your services by offering discounts or incentives.

A strong brand and marketing strategy will help your business grow and expand your reach.

Anticipate Regulatory Changes

The tax landscape is constantly evolving, and staying ahead of new regulations will prevent disruptions to your business.

- **Monitor Legislative Updates:** Keep a close eye on proposed federal, state, and local changes.
- **Participate in Policy Discussions:** Engage with professional groups and lawmakers to influence upcoming tax policies that affect your clients.
- **Adopt a Compliance-First Mindset:** Build internal processes that prioritize compliance with evolving tax laws and prevent future penalties.

By anticipating regulatory changes, you can proactively adjust your services and provide timely advice to clients.

Developing a Long-Term Vision for Growth

Planning for the future is essential to build a sustainable, profitable business. Consider these strategies to position your tax business for long-term success:

- **Create a Five-Year Growth Plan:** Outline specific revenue targets, service expansions, and team-building goals for the next five years.
- **Invest in Leadership Development:** Train and mentor employees to take on leadership roles, enabling you to scale operations.

- **Plan for Succession:** If you plan to retire or sell the business eventually, develop a succession plan to ensure a smooth transition.
- **Embrace Sustainability:** Adopt sustainable practices in your operations to align with growing environmental concerns and attract eco-conscious clients.

A clear vision will keep your business focused on achieving sustainable growth and adapting to future challenges.

Future-Proofing Your Tax Business

The entrepreneurship journey doesn't stop after launching your business—it's an ongoing learning, adapting, and improving process. With a future-focused mindset, your tax business will not only survive but thrive in the years ahead.

Staying ahead requires a proactive approach to industry trends, technology, and client expectations. By embracing innovation, expanding your expertise, and building a resilient business model, you'll position yourself for long-term success. Providing personalized service, investing in brand building, and anticipating regulatory changes will help you stay competitive in an evolving landscape.

Conclusion

Your Path to Success

Starting a tax business offers tremendous opportunities, but success will depend on your ability to adapt, innovate, and deliver exceptional value to your clients. Throughout this book, we've covered every essential step—from laying a strong foundation to mastering industry tools, attracting clients, managing operations, and planning for growth. Each chapter has provide you with practical knowledge and strategies to set you on the right path.

Remember, entrepreneurship is not a one-time event—it's an ongoing journey that requires continuous learning, strategic thinking, and resilience. You may face challenges along the way: evolving tax regulations, shifts in client needs, or market disruptions. However, these obstacles are also opportunities to differentiate yourself from competitors and demonstrate your expertise and reliability.

The key to lasting success lies in building a sustainable business model. Focus on delivering personalized, proactive service, invest in tools and technologies that enhance efficiency, and nurture your client relationships. Stay ahead of industry trends, seek out education and certifications, and always be open to innovation.

Your tax business has the potential to grow beyond your initial vision—whether that means expanding your team, adding new services, or developing a lasting brand.

With the right mindset, discipline, and focus, you can build a profitable enterprise that thrives for years to come. The future is yours to shape—so take that first step and watch your business grow into the success you envision.

Good luck, and here's to your success!

Appendix

1. Essential Resources and Links

- **IRS Tax Resources:**
https://www.irs.gov – Access to official tax forms, updates, and educational tools.
- **National Association of Tax Professionals (NATP):**
https://www.natptax.com – Offers certifications, education, and industry news.
- **QuickBooks Accounting Software:**
https://quickbooks.intuit.com – Accounting tools for bookkeeping and financial tracking.
- **Internal Revenue Service e-Services Portal:**
https://www.irs.gov/e-services – Platform for tax professionals to e-file and manage client accounts.

- **Form 1040:** U.S. Individual Income Tax Return
- **Form 1099:** Income for independent contractors
- **Form W-2:** Wage and tax statement for employees
- **Form 1120:** Corporate tax return
- **Form 1065:** Partnership return

. **Contact Information for Professional Support**

- **IRS Help Line for Tax Professionals:** 1-866-860-4259
- **Small Business Administration (SBA):** 1-800-827-5722
- **NATP Member Support:** support@natptax.com

This appendix provides additional tools and resources to support your journey toward launching and growing a successful tax business. Use these materials to streamline operations, improve client service, and ensure compliancayou scale your enterprise.

www.ingramcontent.com/pod-product-compliance
Lightning Source LLC
Chambersburg PA
CBHW030507220526
45464CB00006B/2692